SPOOKY JOKES

SANDY RANSFORD has been hooked on humour ever since her first job in publishing – editing the jokes for a well-known magazine – and she has now written more joke books than she can count. Born in South Yorkshire (which may account for it), she now lives in rural mid-Wales surrounded by sheep, with her husband, a horse, a cat, two pygmy goats and two miniature ponies – all of which keep her laughing.

JANE ECCLES is a prolific and talented illustrator. She lives in London with her husband, her son Theo and a great many plants. She is also hoping to adopt a rescue cat.

SPOOKY Jokes

Sandy Ransford

ILLUSTRATED BY
Jane Eccles

MACMILLAN CHILDREN'S BOOKS

First published 1999
by Macmillan Children's Books
a division of Macmillan Publishers Ltd
25 Eccleston Place, London SW1W 9NF
Basingstoke and Oxford

Associated companies throughout the world

ISBN 0 330 39061 9

1 3 5 7 9 8 6 4 2

A CIP catalogue record for this book is available from the British Library.

Printed by Mackays of Chatham plc, Chatham, Kent.

Contents

Tomb It May Concern

How does a ghost begin a letter?
'Tomb it may concern.'

How does a ghost keep its feet dry in the rain?
It wears ghouloshes.

What happened to the ghost who was a bad actor?
He was booed off stage.

What do you call a phantom hen?
A poultry-geist.

What do you get if you cross a ghost with a sailor?
A sea-ghoul.

What goes around wailing, wears a white sheet and always points to the north?
A magnetic ghost.

Why did the ghost look in the mirror?
To see if he still wasn't there.

What screams more loudly than a person frightened by a ghost?
Two people frightened by a ghost.

When do ghosts play tricks on each other?
April Ghouls' Day.

How do ghosts cross the Channel?
By hovercraft.

Where do ghosts go in North America?
Lake Eerie.

Where do ghosts like to swim?
In the Dead Sea.

What's a ghost's favourite tree?
A ceme-tree.

What does a ghost put on its face at night?
Vanishing cream.

Knock, knock.
Who's there?
Fred.
Fred who?
Are you Fred of ghosts?

What did the jailer say to the ghost of Charles I?
'You must be off your head.'

A man went to see a medium and told her he'd like to contact the ghost of his dead wife. 'That'll be £50,' replied the medium.

The man gulped. 'Er, can you reverse the charge?' he asked.

What's a ghost's favourite party game?
Haunt the thimble.

What do ghosts who've been in hospital enjoy?
Talking about their apparition.

What do you get if you take a photograph of a ghost?
A transparency.

What do you get if you cross a ghost with a packet of crisps?
Snacks that go crunch in the night.

What did the short-sighted ghost wear?
Spooktacles.

What would you do if a ghost floated through your front door?
Run out of the back door!

Why do ghosts like tall buildings?
They have lots of scarecases.

Why do demons and ghouls get on well together?
Because demons are a ghoul's best friend.

A ghost walked into a pub and asked for a large whisky.
'Sorry,' said the barman, 'I'm afraid we don't serve spirits.'

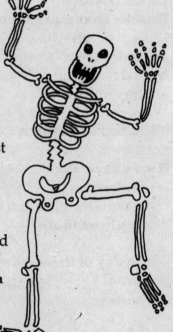

Why was the ghost arrested?
He didn't have a haunting licence.

What's a ghost's least favourite motto?
'Never say die.'

How does a ghost pass through a locked door?
He uses a skeleton key.

What's a ghost's
favourite pub?
**The Horse and
Gloom.**

Where do ghosts
get their jokes from?
Crypt writers.

How do spooks like their
drinks in summer?
Ice ghoul.

Why do spooks like riding horses?
They like ghoulloping.

What do you call a play acted by ghosts?
A phantomime.

What happened when the boy ghost met the
girl ghost?
It was love at first fright.

What does the phantom sentry say?
'Who ghost there?'

Which day of the week is a ghost's
favourite?
Moanday.

BENNY: There's a horror at
the cinema this week.
**JENNY: I know — I
daren't buy a
ticket from her.**

NEW BOY: Is this
school haunted?
**OLD BOY: I don't
think so. Why do
you ask?**
NEW BOY: The teachers
are always talking
about the school spirit.

YOUNG GIRL
GHOST: I
think I'm too
thin.
**YOUNG BOY GHOST: Why do you
say that?**
YOUNG GIRL GHOST: You can see right
through me.

YOUNG GIRL GHOST: Do you believe in
the hereafter?
YOUNG BOY GHOST: Of course.
YOUNG GIRL GHOST: Well, hereafter leave
me alone.

What's a ghost's favourite country?
Wails.

What does a ghost get when he retires?
A ghould watch.

How can you recognise a ghost's bicycle?
By the spooks in its wheels.

Why couldn't the ghost stand up?
He had no visible means of support.

What's it called when a ghost makes a
mistake?
A boo-boo.

What's a ghost's favourite TV programme?
Horror-nation Street.

How do worried ghosts
look?
Grave.

How do you flatten a
ghost?
**With a spirit
level.**

What kind of music does a ghost enjoy?
A haunting melody.

'Doctor, doctor, I keep thinking I'm a ghost.'
**'I wondered why you walked in
through the wall.'**

Why was the ghost admitted to hospital?
**To have his ghoulstones
removed.**

What do you call a
drunken ghost?
**A methylated
spirit.**

Dead Reckoning

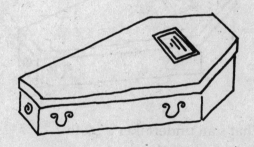

How does an undertaker work out the cost
of a funeral?
By dead reckoning.

Where does an undertaker work?
In a box office.

How does an undertaker fasten his tie?
With a wreath knot.

What's an undertaker's favourite town?
Gravesend.

What's an undertaker's motto?
The morgue the merrier.

BRIAN: I hear you buried your grandad last
week.
**RYAN: Yes, we had to, he was dead,
you know.**

Why did the authorities put a fence round the cemetery?
People were dying to get in.

ADVERT IN NEWSPAPER:
1950s' hearse for sale. Original body.

How can you keep from dying?
Stay in the living-room.

What does a ghoul say when he enters a mortuary?
'Is anybody there?'

PATIENT: Doctor, doctor, I've only got 59 seconds to live!
DOCTOR: Just wait there a minute.

FIRST TAXI-DRIVER: I get tired of my passengers telling me what to do, don't you?

SECOND TAXI-DRIVER: It was all right in my old job. I did it for 20 years and never heard a word of complaint from the back seat.

FIRST TAXI-DRIVER: What did you drive?

SECOND TAXI-DRIVER: A hearse.

What's the difference between a shroud and a person?

One I wear, the other I was.

Why can you never trust an undertaker?

Because one day he'll let you down.

LARRY: When I die I'm going to leave my brain to science.

BARRY: Well, I suppose every little helps.

Lady Jane Grey
Had little to say.
What could she have said
After losing her head?

GRAFFITI ON THE CEMETERY WALL:
Death is Nature's way of telling you to
slow down.

What is it that the man who buys does not
use himself, the man who makes it does not
need, and the person who uses it does so
without knowing?
A coffin.

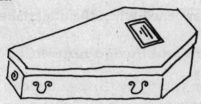

Dr Guillotine invented an excellent cure for
dandruff.

What's the difference between a musician
and a corpse?
One composes; the other decomposes.

CORONER: You say your first and second
wives died after eating poisonous fungi, and
your third was knocked down by a bus. It
seems a bit odd, doesn't it?
MAN: Not really. She wouldn't eat the
fungi.

What's an
undertaker's
favourite saying?
**'Every shroud
has a silver
lining.'**

What happened when the undertaker
retired?
**He went and buried himself in the
country.**

DARREN: Shall I tell you the joke about the
body-snatchers?
SHARON: Oooh, yes.
DARREN: On second thoughts I'd better
not, you might get carried away.

'Doctor, doctor, I'm at death's door!'
**'Don't worry, I'll soon pull you
through.'**

What do undertakers call a funeral parlour?
The departure lounge.

Why can't you be lonely in a graveyard?
There's always some body there.

FIRST GARDENER: We had 50 staff when I worked at the Earl of Huntingdon's.
SECOND GARDENER: I used to work with hundreds under me, not 50!
FIRST GARDENER: Where was that, then?
SECOND GARDENER: The local cemetery.

MAN ON PHONE: Have you got a box for six, please?
REPLY ON PHONE: Sorry, sir, we only have boxes for one.
MAN ON PHONE: Is that the Lyceum Theatre?
REPLY ON PHONE: No, sir, it's Smith Bros, Undertakers.

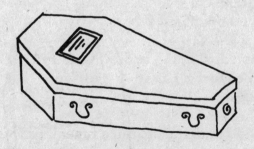

What's an undertaker's favourite outing?
The Hearse of the Year Show.

How can you recognise an undertaker?
By his grave manner.

SIGN ON A TOMBSTONE:
Here lies our MP. He's lying still.

SIGN ON A DENTIST'S TOMBSTONE:
Stranger, approach this spot with gravity, John Smith's filling his last cavity.

SIGN ON YET ANOTHER TOMBSTONE:
He died from drinking varnish. He had a lovely finish.

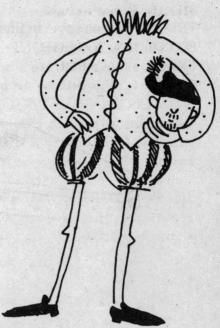

What do you
get when your head is
chopped off?
A splitting headache.

FLICK: I hear you went to see a spiritualist.
Was she any good?
NICK: Oh, medium.

Is it difficult to bury an elephant?
Yes, it's a huge undertaking.

TRIXIE: Au revoir.
DIXIE: What's that?
TRIXIE: It's 'goodbye' in French.
DIXIE: Oh. Arsenic.
TRIXIE: What's that?
DIXIE: It's 'goodbye' in any language.

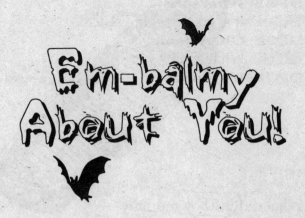

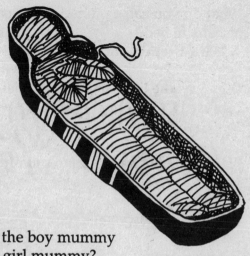

What did the boy mummy
say to the girl mummy?
'Em-balmy about you!'

How can you tell if a mummy is angry?
He flips his lid.

What do mummies wear on their
fingernails?
Nile varnish.

What did the mummy say to her son as she
sent him off to school?
'Wrap up well, dear.'

Why are mummies good with secrets?
They keep everything under wraps.

What do you call a mummy who eats
biscuits in bed?
A crumby mummy.

Why was the little ancient Egyptian boy
confused?
Because his daddy was a mummy.

SHEILA: I met an Egyptian mummy.
LEILA: What did it say?
SHEILA: I don't know, I
don't speak dead languages.

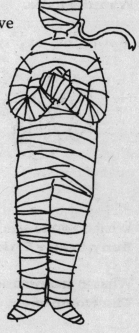

Why did the mummy leave
his tomb?
**After 5,000 years he
thought he was old
enough to leave
home.**

Mrs Mummy was
making arrangements to
have some groceries
delivered. 'I'll probably
be busy when you
arrive,' she told the
delivery man, 'so just
drive up to the door, toot
and come in.'

What do you call a friendly skeleton?
A bony crony.

How do you make a skeleton laugh?
Tickle his funny bone.

How did the skeleton know there would be a thunderstorm?
He could feel it in his bones.

What do you get if you cross a skeleton with a python?
A rattlesnake.

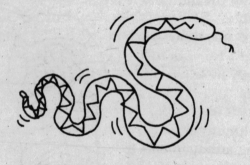

What do you call a skeleton in a kilt?
Bony Prince Charlie.

What instrument does a skeleton play?
The trombone.

FIRST SKELETON: If we had any guts we'd get out of here.
SECOND SKELETON: Yes, but we have no body to help us.

What do you call a skeleton that does no work?
Lazy bones.

What's a definition of noise?
A skeleton dancing on a tin roof.

Which skeleton was emperor of France?
Napoleon Bone-apart.

What did the skeleton say to his girlfriend?
'I love every bone in your body.'

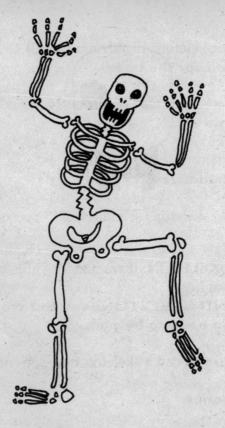

What was Yorick's nickname at school?
Numbskull.

Why don't skeletons go to discos?
They have no body to dance with.

Why was the skeleton no good at his job?
His heart wasn't in it.

Why do skeletons like drinking milk?
It's good for the bones.

What's a skeleton's favourite vegetable?
Marrow.

Who sailed the phantom ship?
A skeleton crew.

What do skeletons sell at fetes?
Rattle tickets.

What should
you do if you
see a skeleton
jogging?
**Jump out of
your skin
and join him!**

Why don't many
skeletons jog?
**They can't
stand the
noise.**

What's a skeleton's favourite song?
'Shake, Rattle and Roll.'

What do you call a detective skeleton?
Sherlock Bones.

When do a skeleton's teeth chatter?
When he's chilled to the marrow.

Bloodbath

What's red and
very silly?
A blood clot.

What do vampires
take before going to
bed?
A bloodbath.

Why did Dracula employ young vampires?
He liked new blood in the business.

How do vampires travel?
By blood vessel.

What do you call a short vampire?
A pain in the leg.

What wears a black cape, flies around at night and sucks blood?
A mosquito in a black cape.

What's a vampire's favourite dance?
The fangdango.

What did the vampire say when the barber cut his neck?
'Never mind, it's not my blood.'

FIRST VAMPIRE: Are you related to Dracula?
SECOND VAMPIRE: Yes, he's a blood relative!

What's a vampire's favourite fruit?
A blood orange.

What's a vampire's favourite soup?
Scream of tomato.

What do vampires do at 11am each day?
Take a coffin break.

Where does Dracula keep his money?
In a blood bank.

Why couldn't Mrs Dracula ever leave
Dracula?
She couldn't bear to kiss him goodbye.

What do vampire pop fans do?
Form a fang club.

YOUNG VAMPIRE: Am I a real vampire,
Mummy?
MOTHER VAMPIRE: Of course, dear.
YOUNG VAMPIRE: Are you sure?
**MOTHER VAMPIRE: Yes, dear. Why
do you ask?**
YOUNG
VAMPIRE:
Because I faint
when I see blood.

What do you get if
you cross a vampire
with a carnation?
**A flower that goes for your throat
when you sniff it.**

What do baby vampires say at bedtime?
'Read me a gory.'

What do vampires like for breakfast?
Ready Neck.

Why is it easy to trick a vampire?
Because they're all suckers.

How does Dracula keep fit?
He plays batminton.

What comes out at night and goes bite, bite, ouch!?
A vampire with toothache.

Why did the vampire carry his coffin with him?
Because his life was at stake.

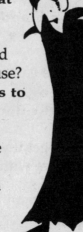

Why is a vampire a good guest to have in the house?
Because he eats necks to nothing.

Can a toothless vampire bite?
No, but he can give a nasty suck.

'Mummy, what's a vampire?'
'Shut up and drink your soup before it clots.'

How do you join Dracula's fan club?
Send your name, address and blood group.

Where does Dracula stay in New York?
The Vampire State Building.

What's a vampire's favourite dessert?
Leeches and scream.

What's a vampire's favourite slogan?
'Please give blood generously.'

Whom did the vampire marry?
The girl necks door.

What do you get if you cross a vampire with the Abominable Snowman?
Frostbite.

Why are vampires crazy?
Because they're bats.

What happened when the boy
vampire met the girl vampire?
It was love at first bite.

What did the polite vampire say to the
dentist after having a tooth filled?
'Fangs a lot.'

What do vampires eat with bread and
cheese?
Pickled organs.

What fruit do vampires buy at the
greengrocer's?
Neck-tarines.

Count Dracula had been seen around with a
very pretty young girl vampire, and he was
asked by a newspaper reporter if this meant
that wedding bells would be ringing soon.
'Oh no,' replied Dracula, 'we're just good
fiends.'

What did a vampire
call a set of dentures?
A new-fangled device.

What do you get if you
cross a vampire with a
telescope?
A horror-scope.

What's the best way to talk to
a vampire?
On the phone.

What was Dracula
before he married?
A bat-chelor.

What would you do if you saw Dracula, a
werewolf, a monster and a skeleton walking
down the road?
**Hope they were going to a fancy dress
party!**

What's pink, has a curly tail and drinks
blood?
A hampire.

What's a vampire's favourite song?
'Fangs For the Memory.'

Why did Dracula eat mints?
He had bat breath.

What was Dracula's favourite dance?
The last vaults.

Why was Dracula sad?
He loved in vein.

If Dracula knocked out his opponent in a boxing match what would his opponent be?
Out for the Count.

FIRST VAMPIRE: Last time I was in London a tramp stopped me and said he hadn't had a bite for days.
SECOND VAMPIRE: What did you do?
FIRST VAMPIRE: I bit him.

Why did the vampire's wife leave him?
He was a pain in the neck.

Where do vampires live?
In a far-off terror-tory.

HATTIE: What did you think of that Dracula film?
MATTIE: It was fang-tastic!

ANDY: Did you hear about the vampire's bike that went round in circles biting people?
MANDY: No, what was it called?
ANDY: A vicious cycle.

'Mummy, Mummy, what's a werewolf?'
'Shut up, Angela, and comb your face.'

How does a werewolf sign a letter?
'Best vicious.'

What did the werewolf say to his victims?
'It's been nice gnawing you.'

MOTHER WEREWOLF: Andrew, go and
check on the baby, he's howling again.

Did you hear about the stupid werewolf that
lay down to chew on a bone? When it got up
again it only had three legs.

Who wrote *A Werewolf's Life*?
Norah Bone.

What happened to the werewolf that fell
into the washing-machine?
It became a wash 'n' werewolf.

What do you call a werewolf that likes to
sleep with the windows open?
A fresh air fiend.

A man went into a bar and ordered a glass
of beer. He was enjoying drinking it when
he noticed a werewolf sitting watching him
from the corner. As he looked at it, the
werewolf began to snarl.

'Er, excuse me,' said the man to the
barman,'is that werewolf safe?'

'Well,' replied the barman,'he's a whole
lot safer than you are.'

Where did the monster have her hair done?
The ugly parlour.

Billy and Gilly were exploring when they
discovered a deep, dark cave. Deeper and
deeper they went, and darker and darker it
got. 'I don't like this much,' said Gilly. 'Will
you hold my hand?'

'Of course,' said Billy, reaching out his
own hand. 'But take that bristly glove off
first.'

'What glove?' asked
Gilly. 'I'm not
wearing
gloves.'

Who brings
monsters'
babies?
The frankenstork.

How do abominable
snowmen dance?
**Snow, snow, quick,
quick, snow.**

What's a monster's favourite football team?
Slitherpool.

GWEN: Have you seen an abominable snowman?
KEN: Not yeti.

FRANKENSTEIN'S MONSTER: I've just had the bolts taken out of my neck.
HIS FRIEND: Really? Have a scar?
FRANKENSTEIN'S MONSTER: No thanks, I don't smoke.

What's big and green and sits in the corner all day looking miserable?
The Incredible Sulk.

How does
Frankenstein eat
his dinner?
He bolts it down.

What did the sea
monster say when
it saw a
submarine?
**'Oh, good,
more tinned
food.'**

MONSTER PATIENT: Do my tests show I'm
normal?
**MONSTER DOCTOR: Oh, yes, both
your heads are quite all right.**

What did Frankenstein say when he was
struck by lightning?
'Phew, I needed that.'

What happened
when the frozen
monster ate a stick
of dynamite?
**He blew his
cool.**

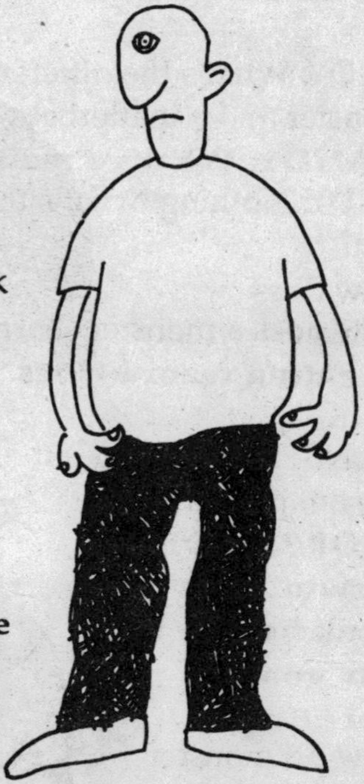

Why did the
cyclops give up
teaching?
**He only had one
pupil.**

What did the
monster eat
after the dentist took out his teeth?
The dentist.

What's a monster's favourite ballet?
Swamp Lake.

Why did the monster give up boxing?
He didn't want to spoil his looks.

How do monsters count up to 100?
On their fingers.

ANDY: What's the difference between a monster and a matterbaby?
MANDY: What's a matterbaby?
ANDY: Nothing, what's the matter with you?

How does a monster sharpen its appetite?
By eating razor blades.

MONSTER: A cup of rat poison, please.
PROPRIETOR: Certainly, sir, to drink here or to take away?

How do monster snowmen feel when they melt?
Abominable.

Who has feathers, fangs and quacks?
Count Duckula.

YOUNG BOY MONSTER: That girl rolled her eyes at me.
HIS FRIEND: Well, roll them back, she might need them.

Why do monsters forget what you tell them?
Because it goes in one ear and out the others.

What do you call a beautiful, clean, well-behaved monster?
A failure.

Frankenstein was unhappy until he learned how to make new friends.

What's a monster's favourite motto?
'Home is where you hang your head.'

Which monster was president of France?
Charles de Ghoul.

How do zombies like their shepherd's pie?
Made with real shepherds.

Why do dragons sleep in the daytime?
So they can fight knights.

Why did Frankenstein go to a psychiatrist?
Because he thought everyone loved him.

FIRST ZOMBIE: You look tired.
SECOND ZOMBIE: Yes, I'm dead on my feet.

What monster lives in your nose?
A bogeyman.

What does a monster do if he has flat feet?
Uses a foot pump.

FIRST MONSTER: Why have you tied a knot in your neck?
SECOND MONSTER: I didn't want my cold to go to my chest.

How does Frankenstein's monster sit in front of the TV?
Bolt upright.

Why is Frankenstein fun to be with?
He has you in stitches.

Who does a zombie take to the cinema?
Any old friend he can dig up.

Why did the monster get good marks in his exam?
Because two heads are better than one.

How can you tell if there's a monster in your fridge?
You can't shut the door.

YOUNG GIRL MONSTER: Why do you say your boyfriend has pedestrian eyes?
HER FRIEND: They look both ways before they cross.

What should you say when you meet a three-headed monster?
'Hello, hello, hello.'

What did the zombie ask the undertaker?
'Do you deliver?'

MOTHER MONSTER: Now, Samantha, don't eat with your fingers. Use a shovel like I taught you.

Which monster runs round Paris in a plastic bag?
The lunch-pack of Notre Dame.

How do you raise a baby monster?
With a fork-lift truck.

What do sea monsters like for supper?
Fish and ships.

Spook When You're Spooken To

What do teachers say to young ghosts at school?
'Only spook when you're spooken to.'

Where does a ghost train stop?
At a manifestation.

What do ghosts eat for breakfast?
Dreaded wheat.

Which ghost has the best hearing?
The eeriest.

How does a ghost count to ten?
One, boo, three, four, five, six, seven, hate, nine, frighten!

What is the title of a famous parliamentary ghost?
The Spooker of the House of Commons.

Knock, knock.
Who's there?
Spectre.
Spectre who?
'Spectre of police, you're under arrest.

What's it called when ghosts star in a TV show?
A spooktacular.

What game do ghosts play at parties?
Haunt and seek.

Where were the ghosts when the lights went out?
In the dark.

MOLLY: Why did Milly marry a ghost?
POLLY: She didn't know what possessed her.

GLORIA GHOST: Will I lose my looks as I get more invisible?
GARY GHOST: I hope so.

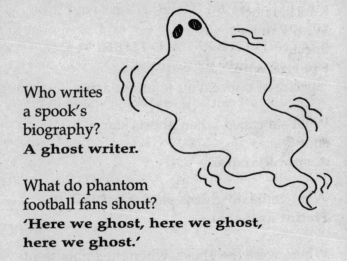

Who writes
a spook's
biography?
A ghost writer.

What do phantom
football fans shout?
**'Here we ghost, here we ghost,
here we ghost.'**

FIRST GHOST: You seem rather depressed.
What's the matter?
**SECOND GHOST: I don't seem to
frighten people any more.**
FIRST GHOST: I know. We might as well be
alive for all they care.

Who keeps a watch for ghost ships?
The ghost guard.

Where do ghosts go on their holidays?
The Ghosta Brava.

What do you call ghost children?
Boys and ghouls.

FIRST GHOST MOTHER: Hasn't your little girl grown!
SECOND GHOST MOTHER: Yes, she's certainly gruesome.

What do you call a ghost with a spade in his head?
Doug.

What did one ghost say to the other?
'I'm sorry but I just don't believe in people.'

The ghost teacher was talking to her class. 'Now, children, did you understand that?' she asked. 'If not, watch the board and I'll go through it again.'

FIRST GHOST: I'm glad I'm not alive today.
SECOND GHOST: Why's that?
FIRST GHOST: There'd be so much more history to learn.

What jewels do ghosts wear?
Tombstones.

How do ghosts keep fit?
By regular exorcize.

Knock, knock.
Who's there?
Hugo.
Hugo who?
Hugo first, I'm
frightened.

What would
you find in the
cellar of a haunted
house?
**Whines and
spirits.**

What did the
young ghost call
his mum and dad?
Transparents.

How did the invisible
child upset her mother?
She kept appearing.

What's a corpse's final drink?
His bier.

What did the young ghost like to chew?
BOOble gum.

What do you call a ghost shepherdess?
Little Boo Peep.

What do ghosts do on holiday?
Have a wail of a time.

How do ghosts repair their shrouds?
By invisible mending.

Why do some ghosts not play the harp?
It takes a lot of pluck.

Who might you meet on a ghost train?
The ticket inspectre.

What walks through a wall and
goes oooob?
**A ghost walking
backwards.**

FIRST GHOST: You give
me eerie ache.
**SECOND GHOST:
Sorry I spook.**

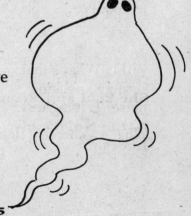

What do
ghosts eat
with roast
beef?
Grave-y.

Why did the fat old ghost sit in a chair
sighing?
She'd lost her ghoulish good looks.

JOHN: Did you hear about the man who
didn't know the meaning of the word fear?
DON: No, why was that?
JOHN: He was too scared
to ask.

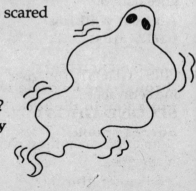

WILL: What's that
strange knocking
noise? Is it a ghost?
**GILL: No, it's my
knees.**

What do ghosts like
for dinner?
Ghoulash.

How does a spook
travel around the
world?
**From ghost to
ghost.**

What does a
ghost take when it has a cough?
Coffin drops.

FIRST GHOST: How did you get that bump
on the head?
**SECOND GHOST: I was floating
through the keyhole when someone
put a key in the lock.**

Who appears on the cover of horror
magazines?
The cover ghoul.

What do
you call a
ghost that
haunts a
hospital?
**A surgical
spirit.**

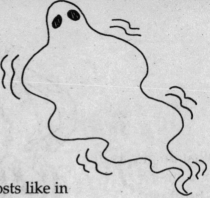

What do ghosts like in
their coffee?
Evaporated milk.

Why did the headless horseman take a bag
of oats to bed with him?
To feed his nightmares.

What's a gargoyle?
**Something a monster takes when it
gets a sore throat.**

What does a ghost fish for?
Angel fish.

Why is it foolish to upset a cannibal?
You might find yourself in hot water.

What do cannibals give their guests?
Pot luck.

What did the cannibal chief say when a parachutist landed in his pot?
'There's a flyer in my soup!'

FIRST CANNIBAL WIFE: I just don't know what to make of my husband.
SECOND CANNIBAL WIFE: How about a stir-fry?

What happened when
the cannibals ate the
comedian?
**They had a
feast of
fun.**

What's a
cannibal's favourite party game?
Swallow my leader.

What's the definition of a cannibal?
**A man who goes into a restaurant and
orders the waiter.**

On which day of the week do cannibals eat
people?
Chewsday.

What did the cannibal say when he spotted
the sleeping man?
'Ah, breakfast in bed.'

What did the cannibal say to the explorer?
'Dr Livingstone, I consume.'

How can you help a starving cannibal?
Give him a hand.

What happened when a cannibal swallowed a watch?
He found it time-consuming.

What do cannibals do at a wedding?
Toast the bride and groom.

Why was the cannibal secretary sacked?
She kept buttering up the boss.

How does a cannibal greet a guest?
'Pleased to eat you.'

'Mummy, mummy, why is daddy so tough?'
'Never mind, dear, leave him and just eat your vegetables.'

FIRST CANNIBAL: I don't like our new neighbour, do you?
SECOND CANNIBAL: No, not really. Try adding more salt and pepper.

FIRST CANNIBAL: Does your wife cook by gas or electricity?
SECOND CANNIBAL: I don't know, I've never tried to cook her.

Is a cannibal who eats his father's sister an aunt-eater?

FIRST CANNIBAL: Who was that lady I saw you with last night?
SECOND CANNIBAL: That was no lady, that was my supper.

Why should you keep calm when introduced to a cannibal?
It's no use getting into a stew.

A cannibal went on a luxury cruise. When the waiter asked him if he would like to see the menu at dinner on the first night, he declined. 'No thanks,' he said, 'just bring me the passenger list.'

FIRST CANNIBAL: You seem a bit down, have you lost your appetite?
SECOND CANNIBAL: No, I'm just a bit fed up with people.

What did the mother cannibal say to her son?
'Don't play with your food.'

FIRST CANNIBAL: We had burglars last night.
SECOND CANNIBAL: Were they any good?
FIRST CANNIBAL: Not bad, but I prefer ship-wrecked sailors.

What happened when the two cannibals fought?
They made mincemeat of each other.

'Waiter, waiter, there's a hand in my soup!'
'That's not your soup, that's your finger bowl.'

What happened to the cannibal after he ate the comedian?
He got a funny feeling in the pit of his stomach.

'How do you know our visitor has been eaten?'
'I have inside information.'

What kind of beans do cannibals like?
Human beans.

Did you hear about the two cannibals who went to a lecture? It was entitled 'How to Serve Your Fellow Man.'

'Mummy, are you sure this is how you make a curry?'
'Shut up and get back in the oven.'

Why did the cannibal push his father into a hot oven?
He wanted snap, crackle and pop.

Why did the cannibal push his father into the deep freeze?
He wanted iced pop.

That's The Spirit!

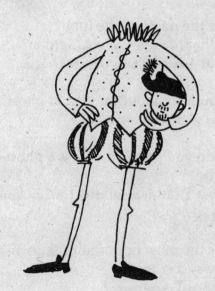

What do
Italian ghosts
eat for lunch?
Spookhetti.

What's the name of the tubby
ghost that haunts Covent Garden?
The fat-tum of the opera.

Did you hear about the stupid ghost?
It climbed over walls.

What do you get if you cross a ghost with a
boy scout?
**A ghost that scares old ladies across
the road.**

What's the most important player in the
spooky soccer team?
The ghoul-keeper.

Where do ghosts send their laundry?
To the dry-screamers.

How did the ghost travel to America?
It took off from Heathrow on a night fright.

How do ghosts keep their feet dry in the rain?
They wear boooots.

What do spooks like to ride on at the fun-fair?
The roller-ghoster.

Why did the ghost steal a purse?
He'd heard the change would do him good.

What do you call a ghost with a sausage on his head?
A head-banger.

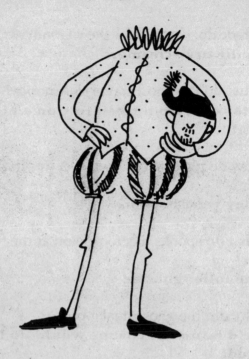

Why did the teacher tell off the young ghosts in her class?
They kept making ghouls of themselves.

What's a guillotine?
A pain in the neck.

How did the dentist become a brain surgeon?
His drill slipped.

Why did Henry VIII have so many wives?
He liked to chop and change.

What do you call two corpses in a belfry?
Dead ringers.

What's a gallows?
A place where no noose is good noose.

What did the executioner write at Christmas?
His chopping list.

A murderer was sitting in an electric chair awaiting execution when the prison governor came in and asked him if he had any last request. 'Yes,' replied the prisoner, 'will you hold my hand?'

Another prisoner who was awaiting execution was asked if he had any last request. 'Yes,' he replied, 'I'd like to sing a song.'

'Go ahead,' said his jailer.

'Right,' said the prisoner. And he began, 'There were nine hundred and ninety-nine thousand, nine hundred and ninety-nine green bottles hanging on a wall . . .'

MAGGIE: Why do you say your husband came to a bitter end?
AGGIE: He drowned in a barrel of beer.

BARBER: Were you wearing a red scarf when you came in?
CUSTOMER: No.
BARBER: Oh dear, I must have cut your throat.

MILLY: Why did you come home early from your farm holiday?
MOLLY: Well, the first day we were there a pig died and we had roast pork for dinner. The second day a calf died and we had roast veal for dinner. The third day a sheep died and we had roast lamb for dinner. The fourth day the farmer died . . . so we left.

PATIENT: I feel half dead.
DOCTOR: That's all right, I'll arrange for you to be buried up to your waist.

PATIENT: Doctor, I feel run down.
DOCTOR: I thought you had tyre marks on your chest.

PASSENGER: A man just fell off the train.
TICKET INSPECTOR: That's all right, he'd paid his fare.

VISITOR: My friend just fell down your well.
FARMER: That's all right, no one drinks from it any more.

WIFE OF SICK HUSBAND: Is there no hope, Doctor?
DOCTOR: It depends what you're hoping for!

Why are ghosts bad at telling lies?
Because you can see right through them.

FIRST GHOST: I had trouble breathing.
SECOND GHOST: What happened?
FIRST GHOST: The doctor gave me
something to stop it.

MARY: Why don't you marry Darren?
**SHARON: He says he'll die if I don't
so I'm waiting to see what happens.**

What's a witch's favourite music?
Hagtime.

MOTHER: Henry! Tell me where you buried your father in the sand, he's got the car keys in his pocket.

'Mummy, mummy, I don't want to go to Australia.'
'Shut up and keep digging.'

'Mummy, mummy. why can't we have a waste disposal unit?'
'Shut up and keep chewing.'

What do ghouls eat for tea?
Baked beings on toast.

Can a man marry his widow's sister?
No, he'd have to be dead to have a widow.

What do you give a witch at teatime?
A cup and sorcerer.

Where do you find zombies' nails?
At the end of zombies' fingers.

Why couldn't the witch talk on the phone?
She had a frog in her throat.

Why couldn't the young witch write a
proper letter?
She hadn't learnt to spell.

Why do witches ride broomsticks?
Vacuum cleaners are too heavy to fly.

What do you call a nervous sorceress?
A twitch.

DOCTOR: First the bad news – I'm afraid
your husband has passed away. Now the
good news – the man in the next-door bed
wants to buy his slippers.

What did the doctor say to the invisible
man?
'I can see you're not all there.'

What do you call a monster with six eyes
and three mouths?
Very ugly!

Two members of the circus were talking about a former colleague who worked as a magician and whose party piece was sawing people in half. 'An odd fellow,' remarked a clown. 'Was he an only child?'

'Oh, no,' replied the elephant trainer. 'I believe he had lots of half brothers and sisters.'

How can you tell if someone has a glass eye?
When it comes out in conversation.

What's a ghost rider's favourite sport?
Fox haunting.

YOUNG GHOST: How does it feel to hurtle through doors and walls?
OLD GHOST: It hurtles!

A ghost was moaning about being unemployed. 'You could always do charity work,' said his friend.

'Such as?' enquired the ghost.

'Well, you could go round scaring people out of their hiccups,' replied the friend.

What happened to the man who refused to pay an exorcist's bill?
He was repossessed.

Two ghosts were discussing their future.
'What happens if you've been good in life?'
asked the first.

'You live in everlasting bliss,' replied the
second.

'And what if you were bad?' asked the
first.

'Then you live with everlasting blisters,'
replied his friend.

GILL: Do you believe in ghosts?
BILL: No.
GILL: I dare you to spend the night in a
haunted house, then. Will you?
BILL: No.
GILL: Why not? If
you don't believe
in ghosts?
**BILL: Well, I
don't believe in
them, but I
might be wrong.**

What's transparent, goes boo and has eight wheels?
A ghost on roller skates.

Why did the ghost's trousers fall down?
Because they had no visible means of support.

Why did the undertaker chop up all the bodies?
So they could rest in pieces.

A monster took his zombie friend to the undertaker's. 'I'd like to order a coffin for a friend of mine who has just died,' explained the monster.

'Fine,' said the undertaker. 'But you didn't have to bring him with you.'

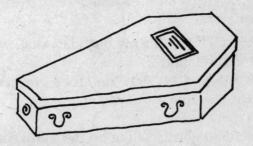

What kind of breakfast cereal do ghosts eat?
Dreaded wheat.

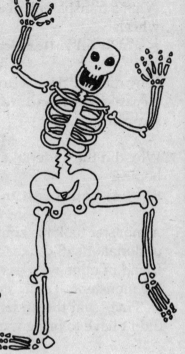

Why don't skeletons
like having baths?
**They're scared of
slipping down the
plughole.**

How do ghosts fly to
America?
**By British
Scareways.**

FIRST GHOST: It's my birthday, shall we go
out and celebrate?
**SECOND GHOST: Yes, let's go out and
paint the town dead.**

Where do ghosts sail to on the south coast?
The Isle of Fright.

Knock, knock.

Who's there?
Donna.
Donna who?
Donna look
now, but there's
a ghost right
behind you . . .

Sandy Ransford

Spooky Puzzles

A spooktacular collection of spooky puzzles.

Sort out which witch is which

Hallowe'en wordsearches

Spot the creepy differences

Ghostly crosswords

Decipher the ghoulish message

Sandy Ransford

2001

A JOKE ODYSSEY

The Millennium Joke Book

2001 side-splittingly funny jokes for the millennium . . .

Why did the lobster blush?
Because the seaweed.

What do cannibals do at a wedding?
Toast the bride and groom.

What can a whole apple do that half an apple can't do?
Look round.

Why was the mushroom invited to lots of parties?
He was a fungi to be with.

Why is a football stadium cool?
Because there's a fan in every seat.

What do you call a vicar on a motorbike?
Rev.

A selected list of titles available from Macmillan and Pan Books

The prices shown below are correct at the time of going to press. However, Macmillan Publishers reserve the right to show new retail prices on covers which may differ from those previously advertised.

SANDY RANSFORD

The Knock Knock Joke Book	0 330 37514 8	£2.99
Football Jokes	0 330 35408 6	£2.99
Spooky Puzzles	0 330 37517 2	£2.99
2001 A Joke Odyssey	0 330 34988 0	£3.99

All Macmillan titles can be ordered at your local bookshop or are available by post from:

Book Service by Post
PO Box 29, Douglas, Isle of Man IM99 1BQ

Credit cards accepted. For details:
Telephone: 01624 675137
Fax: 01624 670923
E-mail: bookshop@enterprise.net

Free postage and packing in the UK.
Overseas customers: add £1 per book (paperback) and £3 per book (hardback).